The Hazards of Strange Bedfellows
The United States, Nigeria, and Peacekeeping in West Africa

Instability in West Africa presents U.S. decision-makers with a conundrum. America's domestic imperative to avoid new entangling commitments abroad is tempered by the CNN effect – the need to "do something" to alleviate the plight of those affected by armed conflict. Responding to these contradictory pressures, successive U.S. administrations have advocated reliance on Africans to maintain peace and security on the continent. This approach, while consistent with Chapter VIII of the United Nations charter, has practical limitations.

This paper is focused on U.S. support for Nigerian military intervention in West Africa, using events in Liberia and Sierra Leone as case studies. The wisdom of working through a regional hegemon to resolve conflict in third countries is examined, as is the utility of peacekeeping itself. The body of this paper is divided into four main parts, dealing with Liberia, Sierra Leone, U.N. peacekeeping, and U.S. foreign policy.

In Liberia's corner of West Africa, demographics and globalization have both contributed to a contagious anarchy.[1] At its heart, however, the spreading instability in the region is not caused by these phenomena, nor is it spontaneous. State sponsorship of insurrection in neighboring states is at the root of the case studies reviewed below. Inappropriate international responses to this combination of invasion and rebellion have only compounded the problems faced.

The U.S. partnership with Nigeria on regional stability issues considerably predates Abuja's transition to democratic governance, although the relationship between the two states was more discreet prior to 1998. When Nigeria's military dictator General

Sani Abacha and his prominent civilian opponent Chief M.K.O. Abiola died of heart attacks in late June and early July 1998 respectively, the curious coincidence set the stage for a return to democracy. General Abdulsalam Abubakr oversaw a Nigerian transitional government, undertaking dramatic political reforms and scheduling an election that took place within a year of Abacha's death. Retired General Olusegun Obasanjo then took the reins of an elected government in May 1999. In the course of consolidating power and reforming the military, Obasanjo undertook sweeping changes in the armed forces. He retired 17 Nigerian Generals in January 2001, and then retired the military's top man, Army Chief of Staff Lieutenant General Malu, three months later.[2] Ensuring the success of Nigeria's fledgling democracy has become a rationale for significant increases in U.S. aid to the Nigerian military. In the rush to assist Abuja, U.S. policymakers frequently cite the Nigerian military's past accomplishments in ensuring regional stability. Nigeria's record in this regard is, however, unfortunately suspect.

The available evidence, outlined below, clearly suggests that U.S. support for the Nigerian military's ongoing operations in West Africa is misguided. Funds, equipment, and training provided to Nigeria profits segments of that country's military, as well as the U.S. contractors involved in the process. American largess does not, however, contribute to regional conflict resolution, and may indeed retard it.

Liberia and the Instigators of Instability

The latest chapter in Liberia's sad history can be traced to Charles Taylor's armed invasion. In December 1989, Taylor, a former Liberian government official who had fled to the U.S. to escape corruption charges, returned to his native Liberia leading a band of about 160 rebel followers. There they confronted the dictatorial regime of Samuel Doe, a

3

former noncommissioned officer who had come to power through a coup in 1980.[3] Taylor's rebel National Patriotic Front of Liberia (NPFL) swelled to 6,000 men within months. With significant materiel support from the government of Burkina Faso,[4] the NPFL gained control of all the major Liberian towns outside of Monrovia by August 1990. Fighting was fierce in the first year of the conflict - an estimated 200,000 people died and an additional 600,000 displaced persons sought refuge in Sierra Leone and Cote D'ivoire.[5]

Events in Liberia were of concern to Nigerian officials for several reasons. Doe, an ally of Nigerian military dictator Major General Ibrahim Babangida, was in a beleaguered position. Taylor, with reputed ties to Libya, also represented a potential threat to stability beyond Liberia's borders. More immediately, three thousand Nigerian citizens residing in Liberia had been rounded up by the NPFL and moved to the country's interior as hostages. The safety of the Nigerian embassy in Monrovia was becoming increasingly precarious as well.

The Economic Community of West African States (ECOWAS), at the suggestion of Babangida, dispatched troops to Liberia in August 1990 to contain the civil war.[6] The newly formed multinational military entity was termed the ECOWAS Ceasefire Monitoring Group (ECOMOG), although there was no ceasefire in effect at the time of its dispatch. The ECOMOG force initially consisted of Nigerians, Ghanaians, Gambians, and Sierra Leonean troops organized in national contingents.[7] Its first overall Force Commander was Ghanaian General Arnold Quainoo, but the overwhelming majority of ECOMOG's troops and key leaders were Nigerian.

From the outset, the Nigerian dominated ECOMOG intervention was perceived by Liberians to be a partisan effort directed against Charles Taylor. NPFL forces that had encircled the city immediately engaged ECOMOG troops on the edge of Monrovia. In a significant incident, Doe was murdered shortly after the arrival of ECOMOG. A splinter group of the NPFL, led by Prince Yomie Johnson, kidnapped Doe from ECOMOG quarters in September 1990 and killed him. This led to the removal of Quainoo as Force Commander, and his replacement by a Nigerian General Dogonyaro. The command of ECOMOG remained in Nigerian hands throughout the remainder of the conflict.

From 1990 to 1992, ECOMOG was able to hold Monrovia, but made little progress in expanding its area of control. A series of thirteen ceasefires between the various warring factions were negotiated in the following years, apparently motivated more by the warring parties' tactical considerations than good faith. As these agreements invariably broke down, ECOMOG's mission alternated between peacekeeping and peace enforcement. ECOMOG forces spread out throughout the Liberian countryside to monitor the ceasefires in times of peace, adopting force posture vulnerabilities that gave the warring factions leverage over them when hostilities renewed. Five hundred ECOMOG peacekeepers were taken hostage in 1992, in an action that presaged similar events in Bosnia and Sierra Leone.

Over time, ECOMOG vacillated between agendas favoring various Liberian factions, to include United Liberation Movement for Democracy in Liberia (ULIMO), ULIMO-K, later ULIMO-J, and ultimately the NPFL. An agreement between Taylor and Babangida cleared the way for Liberian elections and a peace agreement that finally held in 1997. In winning the election, Taylor employed a memorably ominous campaign slogan; "He killed your ma, he killed your pa - vote for Taylor."[8]

Episodes of individual valor among the Nigerian military contingent within ECOMOG during the Liberian contingency were marred by widespread corruption. The priority for many Nigerian troops in ECOMOG, who sometimes went months without being paid, was often on personal profit.[9] Looting by ostensible peacekeepers was common, and quickly led Liberians to suggest that ECOMOG should stand for Every Car Or Movable Object Gone.[10] As ECOMOG's presence in Liberia dragged on over seven years, corruption became institutionalized and ever more efficient. Illicit ECOMOG economic endeavors in Liberia developed, centered on rubber, timber, U.N. humanitarian aid, drugs and diamonds.[11] Criminal profits made sustaining deployment abroad an end unto itself for many in the military.

Domestically, Nigerian involvement in ECOMOG was unpopular. While Nigerians generally accepted their governments' argument that Libyan sponsored instability spreading from Burkina Faso had to be contained, the cost of doing so was perceived as excessive. The Nigerian windfall from oil revenues during the Gulf War was consumed by the ECOMOG deployment.[12] As the Nigerian economy faced harder times in later years, Nigerian deployments abroad became increasingly controversial. Nigerian records put the total spent on ECOMOG by past military governments at $8 billion.[13]

Ultimately, the Nigerian led intervention in Liberia merely delayed a transfer of power from one corrupt despot to another. It neither saved Doe nor stopped Taylor. The arrival of the Nigerians in August 1990 very likely saved residents of Monrovia from

6

starvation. It also, however, kept the factions fighting Taylor fed and armed for years. By prolonging the period in which Liberia was divided without a single sovereign, ECOMOG did little for nation building. The Taylor regime has conformed to expectations since taking power, continuing to incite unrest in neighboring countries. In the recent words of one diplomat, "What you call the West African problem is what I call the Charles Taylor problem. It is not hard to see who is at the root of all this."[14]

Sierra Leone's Complex Complicities

The recent conflict in Liberia is inexorably linked with the one in Sierra Leone. In March 1991, NPFL forces crossed into Sierra Leone from Liberia.[15] Targeting the capture of diamond mining areas, the offensive was led by former Sierra Leone Corporal Foday Sankoh. A close friend of Taylor's, Sankoh had previously attended training with him in Libya and worked together with him in support of Blaise Campaore's coup in Burkina Faso.[16] The Revolutionary United Front (RUF) movement Sankoh founded in Sierra Leone was in many respects an offshoot of the NPFL.

A year after the RUF invasion, the government of Sierra Leone fell to a military coup in April 1992 led by 28-year-old army Captain Valentine Strasser.[17] In 1993, Strasser's National Provisional Ruling Council (NPRC), with the assistance of $18 million in U.S. military aid, was able to regain diamond mines in the south and the east previously lost to the RUF. These gains, however, proved to be short lived. Sierra Leone soldiers themselves began to engage in illegal mining, exporting the diamonds through Liberia as the RUF had. Government revenues remained low and RUF activity based in Liberia picked up. Guinea, countering RUF incursions into diamond-mining regions on its territory, conducted cross-border raids to attack the RUF in Sierra Leone. Further confusing the situation was the emergence of the "Sobel" phenomenon, as more and more Sierra Leone troops became soldiers by day and rebels at night.[18] By 1995, the RUF had taken back the Sierra Leone diamond mines, were in control of the northern half of the country, and were approaching Freetown.

Lacking a credible military force, the Strasser junta hired mercenaries to counter the RUF. In exchange for a promise of future mining revenues, Executive Outcomes (EO), based in South Africa, deployed men to Sierra Leone in May 1995. Using two MI-17 helicopter gunships and a MI-24, EO mercenaries in Sierra Leone uniforms recaptured all the diamond-mining centers within nine months of their arrival.[19] Their military prowess did not, however, save Strasser. He was ousted in a military coup led by Defense Minister Brigadier General Julius Mada Bio in January 1996. Bio arranged for elections as a precursor to a return to civilian rule, and negotiated a ceasefire with the RUF.

Ahmad Tejan Kabbah emerged from the March 1996 elections as the President of Sierra Leone. Upon taking office, he terminated Sierra Leone's relationship with EO, signed a bilateral defense pact with Nigeria, and negotiated a peace agreement with the RUF. The November 1996 agreement, known as the Abidjan Peace Accord, required the RUF to disarm, demobilize, and transform into a political party. The accord was overtaken by events before it could be implemented. On 25 May 1997, Sierra Leone Army Major Johnny Paul Koroma and about 20 confederates stormed a Freetown prison, released approximately 600 prisoners (including two Russians), and overthrew the elected government.[20] Koroma's Armed Forces Revolutionary Council (AFRC) then declared themselves the new rulers of Sierra Leone, and invited the RUF to join them.

The RUF marched into an already anarchic Freetown, and Kabbah fled to Guinea. From his exile in Conakry, Kabbah requested Nigerian intervention under the terms of their bilateral pact. [21] Just as scheduled elections in Liberia heralded the imminent end of one prolonged Nigerian military operation abroad, another beckoned.

ECOMOG headquarters in Monrovia sluggishly planned and executed the overall Nigerian military response to the Sierra Leone coup.[22] Force Commander Lieutenant General Victor Malu, who was away in Nigeria at the time of the coup, took weeks to return. Once back, he took the lead in a dual track strategy of negotiations with the AFRC and simultaneous preparations for a military solution.[23] Western observers present at Malu's talks with the RUF in Freetown subsequently spotted several RUF state ministers from Koroma's cabinet, presumed to be Liberians, frequenting the streets of Monrovia.

The Nigerians and AFRC/RUF agreed to a plan to restore democratic government to Sierra Leone, codified in the Conakry Accord of 23 October 1997.[24] That Accord was, however, never implemented. In February 1998, almost a year after the coup, ECOMOG troops from Nigeria took Freetown from the AFRC/RUF. ECOMOG entered Freetown as they had deployed to Monrovia, not as peacekeepers but as belligerents. Kabbah, restored to power by foreign arms, returned to Freetown profoundly weakened, able to exercise only limited sovereignty. The RUF retained control over most of north of the country, to include its diamond mines. Kabbah's government, in contrast, was virtually trapped in Freetown, lacked sources of recurring income, and had no national Army.[25]

The Nigerians, who had been slow to restore the Kabbah government in Freetown, were also in no hurry to push into the interior of the country. When they did advance in April 1998, Nigerian inexperience at counterinsurgency tactics cost them dearly. The RUF struck back in December 1998, partially overrunning Freetown again. It took ECOMOG over a week to regain full control of the city.

Among those caught up in the December 1998 battle for Freetown was Major General Max Khobe. He narrowly escaped capture when the RUF overran Hastings airfield, and, while wounded, had to evade their forces in hostile territory for days. As a Nigerian Colonel, Khobe had been an ECOMOG brigade commander in Liberia when Malu was Chief of Staff. Once ECOMOG took Freetown following the Koroma coup, Khobe became the Sierra Leone Army Chief of Defense Staff. One of his primary duties was to recreate a Sierra Leone Army, as there were essentially no loyal regime forces following the 1997 coup. Khobe presided over the training of captured rebels who were projected to eventually constitute a new Sierra Leone Army. Three groups of rebels processed through Khobe's camp, and each remained true to Sierra Leone's Sobel tradition. A majority of them deserted, surrendered, or turned on the Nigerians once they were sent to the front. Khobe himself was in many respects typical of Nigerian soldiers deployed to restore stability – a confounding combination of bravery and corruption. He was featured prominently in Indian MG Jetley's unpublished memo to the United Nations (UN) in September 2000:

> "(T)he Nigerian army was interested in staying in Sierra Leone due to the massive benefits they were getting from the illegal diamond mining. Brig Gen Maxwell Khobe was commonly known as the "Ten Million Dollar man," it is alleged that he received up to 10 million dollars to permit the activities of the RUF."[26]

Khobe died around the time of Jetley's memo, reportedly of natural causes.

Diamonds are at the heart of the current conflicts in West Africa, providing the wherewithal to finance Taylor's allies and corrupt the forces that would oppose them.

Cross border incursions into Sierra Leone and Guinea target diamond mining areas which are crucial to the economic well being of those countries. Liberia's main export remains diamonds, a significant number of which originate elsewhere. The bulk of RUF diamond exports, valued at around $75 million annually, continue to leave Sierra Leone through Liberia. The complicity of the Liberian government in this activity has been documented by the United Nations, as has the friction caused by diamonds within the rebel movement.[27]

Many of the RUF's well-publicized atrocities against civilians occurred in the months following their December 1998 offensive against Freetown. Up to 5,000 people were killed by the RUF, and thousands more had their hands, feet, or ears amputated. This period of terror was paralleled by a marked improvement in RUF military tactics. Ukrainian, Burkinabe, Nigerien, Libyan, and South African mercenaries appeared around Gbatala, Liberia to train RUF combatants.[28] The RUF's new tactical sophistication soon made itself felt in ECOMOG casualties, as the Nigerians reported up to 30 deaths a day.[29] The 20,000 Nigerian soldiers in Sierra Leone in early 1999, who constituted nearly a quarter of the entire Nigerian armed forces, were proving unable to defeat the RUF.[30] Discipline among the Nigerians began to break down as the military situation deteriorated. Nigerian troops summarily executed dozens of civilians in January 1999, including children and hospital patients.[31]

Faced with mounting costs associated with the operation in Sierra Leone and an unfavorable military situation on the ground, Nigeria threatened to pull its troops out altogether. [32] Under pressure from multiple foreign benefactors, Kabbah then signed a peace agreement Sankoh (who had been released by the Nigerians) in Lome, Togo on 7

July 1999. The Lome Accord, as it came to be known, granted an absolute pardon to RUF members, made Sankoh Vice President, officially entrusted him with the management of Sierra Leone's strategic resources (diamonds), provided the RUF four cabinet ministries within the government, and called for the disarmament of RUF combatants.[33] It also requested the United Nations Observer Mission in Sierra Leone (UNOMSIL), which had evacuated Freetown in December 1998, return and monitor Lome Accord implementation.

U.N. Peacekeeping – Paradigm Lost?

U.N. military operations enjoyed their heyday between 1988 and 1992. Thirteen peacekeeping and peace enforcement operations were undertaken in that period, as many as in the previous forty years combined.[34] The U.N. operations renaissance came to an end with the deaths of 18 U.S. servicemen in Mogadishu, Somalia on 3 October 1993. That incident resulted in disillusionment with U.N. operations among many developed nations, and led to reluctance within the U.N. to undertake decisive military action. One U.N. official at the time commented, "The U.N. is out of peace enforcement for good."[35]

The number of peacekeepers, and U.N. funding available for them, declined in the mid- and late 1990's, as the developed world largely turned its attentions elsewhere. Whereas 82,000 peacekeepers were deployed in 1993, only 8,000 peacekeepers were fielded in 1995, and fewer than 1000 by 1999. The overall costs of U.N. peacekeeping operations peaked at $4 billion in 1993. That figure declined to $1.4 billion in 1996, to $1.3 billion in 1997, and bottomed out at 900 million in 1998.[36] U.N. Secretary General Boutros Boutros-Ghali, who had engineered the explosion of peacekeeping up to 1993, fought its decline. He reached out to regional organizations,[37] including ECOWAS, asking them to take on active peacekeeping roles in "orphan conflicts" in the developing world.[38]

A U.S. veto prevented Boutros-Ghali from serving a second term as Secretary General, but his legacy of regional peacekeepers remains.[39] Whereas developed nations provided the bulk of peacekeeping soldiers prior to the conclusion of the Cold War, 77% of UN peacekeeping forces fielded in the year 2000 were from developing countries. The top five troop contributing states – India, Nigeria, Jordan, Bangladesh, and Ghana - were all from the developing world.

When the U.N. Security Council endorsed the Lome Accords in Resolution 1260 in August 1999, it authorized the expansion of UNOMSIL to 210 military observers.[40] The Nigerian military, presented with an opportunity to legitimize their efforts with a U.N. imprimatur and also receive U.N. funding, reconsidered its decision to withdraw from Sierra Leone. When a force of 6,000 U.N. Mission in Sierra Leone (UNAMSIL) peacekeepers was authorized by U.N. Resolution 1270 in October 1999, Nigerians formed a large part of the contingent.[41]

In early May 2000, the RUF kidnapped hundreds of U.N. personnel who had deployed to monitor compliance with the Lome Accords.[42] As RUF rebels massed 85 kilometers north of Freetown at Rogberi Junction,[43] the British decided to intervene. With little faith in Nigerians or the U.N. forces, they deployed their own soldiers to Freetown. Operating under a Commonwealth mandate, an advance force of 400 British troops from the Parachute Regiment was flown into Freetown by the Royal Air Force. 800 Royal Marines, aboard the new amphibious assault carrier HMS Ocean, followed them.[44] Quick action ordered by British Brigadier General Richards, to include helicopter assaults on advancing rebels, saved Freetown from falling to the RUF again.

The British, former colonial masters of Sierra Leone, had worked extensively behind the scenes in recent years in support of the elected government there.[45] While the Koroma junta lasted, the UK government paid the expenses of Kabbah's exiled government in Guinea, and also provided for a clandestine radio station in Conakry from which Kabbah could broadcast back to Sierra Leone. At the time of the UK intervention in 1999, the UK was already providing an aid package to Sierra Leone totaling 10 million British pounds.[46] The UK has maintained a military presence in Sierra Leone since May 1999, engaged in both military training and nation building. A British Colonel now works with the Sierra Leone Chief of Defense Staff (Khobe's former position, now occupied by a Sierra Leone national), a British policeman leads the Sierra Leone police force, and a British accountant keeps track of Sierra Leone's public finances.[47] The UK commitment to Sierra Leone, while apparently unending, is also unwavering. Secretary of State Defense Hoon stated recently that British Rapid Deployment Forces would return to Freetown within 24 hours if required.[48]

In contrast to the UK performance in Sierra Leone, UNAMSIL got off to a rough start. Hampered by internal bickering and a fluctuating situation on the ground, the U.N. was quickly caught in the ECOMOG trap of alternating between peacekeeping and peace enforcement.[49] In August 2000, the U.N. extended and expanded UNAMSIL's mandate, authorizing offensive action. The following month, GEN Jetley reported to the U.N. on illegal diamond trading between senior Nigerian military officers and the RUF. Rather than investigate the allegations made by the impolitic UNAMSIL Commander, the U.N.

removed him. India and Jordan, the two most capable militaries within UNAMSIL, then announced that they would withdraw their forces from Sierra Leone.[50] Another tenuous ceasefire was signed in November 2000. UNAMSIL forces today number 12,100, and are scheduled to increase to 17,500 total this summer. The peacekeeping mission cost is estimated to be $1.5 million a day.[51] Even so, many outsider observers place more faith in the 500-man UK force in Sierra Leone than they do in UNAMSIL.

Meanwhile an armed conflict has sprung up in Guinea that illustrates the transnational nature of West African proxy insurgencies, and the futility of trying to contain them in isolation. Over 1,000 people have already been killed this year in the border region between Sierra Leone, Liberia, and Guinea. ECOWAS agreed in December to deploy a 1,700-man force to the area under Nigerian command, but "logistics problems" have delayed its dispatch.[52] At stake are Guinean diamond mines the RUF has tried to take in the past. On the one side of the conflict is Guinea's President Lansana Conte, a troop contributor to ECOMOG and a long-time foe of Charles Taylor. Conte's army has occasionally crossed the Sierra Leone border with helicopter gunships and artillery to inflict heavy casualties on the RUF, most recently in April 2001.[53] Guinea also hosts exiled Liberians from the ULIMO-K faction, who reside primarily near the border towns of Gueckedou and Macenta. A Guinean rebel group based in Liberia crossed the border to briefly occupy those towns in April 2001, but was driven back in heavy fighting. Styling itself "*Rassemblement des Forces Democratiques de Guinee*", the group sponsored by Taylor is headed by Guinean army mutineers who fled their country following a failed coup attempt in 1996. Taylor, who is reportedly mobilizing thousands of Liberians,[54] has insisted that any ECOWAS troops sent to the conflict region be strictly limited to mission of monitoring the situation. Over a decade after Charles

Taylor returned to West Africa, events in Guinea have a familiar ring. What is

remarkable about the methods employed to contend with them is how little they vary

from ineffective responses to instability undertaken in the past.

Declining participation by developed nations in peacekeeping operations is not

entirely attributable to risk aversion or donor fatigue. The very utility of peacekeeping is

in doubt. As the prevalent form of international conflict at the close of the twentieth

century evolved from wars between states to wars within states, the conflict resolution

methods envisioned in the aging U.N. charter lost their currency.[55] The ground rules for

implementing peacekeeping, designed for inter-state war, are often inappropriate in a

civil war context. U.N. peacekeeping practice requires the consent of all parties in a

conflict before troops are deployed, the impartiality of U.N. troops once on the ground,

and the use of force by U.N. troops only in self-defense. Studies indicate, however, that

governments lose their legitimacy when they negotiate with rebels, and peace settlements

emerging from such negotiations seldom last. [56] There are rare cases where unique

circumstances allow peacekeeping to succeed. Mozambique is one of few exceptional

cases where peacekeeping actually proven useful. Generally, however, peacekeeping

endures as a practice not because it works, but because its alternatives have been

perceived as worse.

Troops on U.N. peacekeeping missions in recent years, restricted to acting in self-

defense, have frequently confused their mandate of impartiality with neutrality. The

result has too often been a UN military force prone to appeasing aggressors, and poorly

suited to overseeing true disarmament, demobilization, and reintegration of former combatants.[57] Equally damning, the duration of UN deployments has proved difficult to curtail. The fifty years UN observers have been present in Cyprus, the Middle East, and India/Pakistan belies any illusion that peacekeeping alone is an effective solution to conflict. Inertia takes on new immediacy in civil war contexts, where prolonging the "temporary" division of states undermines domestic and international stability.

U.S. Foreign Policy – Noblesse Oblige?

Within West Africa, Liberia's unique history ties it to America like no other country. Samuel Doe, who took power through the murder of President Tolbert, became the first Liberian head of state in modern times that was not descended from American slaves. His violent seizure of power in 1980, however, had no substantial impact on Liberia's relationship with its benefactor. Doe, like his predecessors, was sustained in large part by U.S. government patronage. Liberia was the recipient of the highest per capita U.S. government aid of any country in Sub-Saharan Africa under Doe. American assets in Liberia included an Omega navigation station, which transmitted communications to submarines in the South Atlantic, a Voice of America transmitter that broadcast to all of sub-Saharan Africa, and a strong CIA regional presence.[58] Prior to the war with the NPFL, almost 5,000 Americans resided in Liberia.[59]

Despite a 500-man U.S. embassy in Monrovia, Taylor's rise to power took Washington by surprise. His rapid transition from the leader of a small band of followers to the warlord controlling most of Liberia's countryside can be credited in large part to the ineptness of the Doe regime. It was also Doe's flaws, so apparent over years of waste and corruption, which made many in Washington hesitate to come to his aid. Atrocities committed by government forces as they battled Taylor's rebels in Nimba province also made publicly taking sides difficult, despite U.S. ties to the regime in Monrovia. There were no lack of National Security Council (NSC) meetings in Washington DC focused on Liberia, at the Principals and Deputies Committee levels, in early 1990. Decisive American action, however, was not forthcoming. Nor was there a public outcry for it. CNN provided some reporting on the horrific early months of the war, but media coverage of Liberia in the developed world dissipated when Iraq invaded Kuwait.

The Bureau of African Affairs at the State Department had formulated detailed plans to effect peaceful regime change in Liberia in the spring of 1990. State proposed exiling Doe to Togo, inviting Taylor to join an "all parties" interim Liberian government, and then transitioning to elections that same year. The concept was coordinated with Togo's President, official contact was taken up with NPFL representatives, and U.S. Charge d'affaires in Monrovia, Dennis Jett, started mentally preparing Doe to leave Liberia. This process was brought to an abrupt halt in June 1990, when the NSC directed that the U.S. would not "take charge of the Liberian problem."[60] Chairman of the NSC Deputies Committee, Robert Gates, had concluded that the U.S. had no vital interests in Liberia. Woefully understaffed on Africa issues, the NSC attached little weight to historic ties between the U.S. and Liberia.[61] National Security Advisor Brent Scowcroft later stated that he had feared direct U.S. involvement in settling the crisis might have created an expectation that U.S. troops would serve as peacekeepers in Liberia.[62]

Actions taken by the U.S. military at the outset of the crises in West Africa were restricted to Noncombatant Evacuation Operations (NEO), managed by the U.S. European Command (EUCOM). From April 1990 to January 1991, EUCOM Operation Sharp Edge evacuated U.S. persons from Liberia. A similar operation, put together so hastily that it was not assigned a name, evacuated U.S. persons from Sierra Leone from 29 April 92 to 4 May 1992.

As U.S. decision-makers resolved to stay out of the region's conflicts, they rushed to find surrogates who would get involved. Senegal agreed to deploy troops to Liberia as part of ECOMOG in return for $15 million in U.S. aid in 1991. Another $19 million was provided to Kenya and Tanzania in 1993 and 1994. The chief hurdle U.S. policymakers had in their efforts to assist West Africans in containing Charles Taylor was Babangida's decision to annul the 12 June 1993 Nigerian elections. In response to Babangida's action, the U.S. joined other Western nations in imposing sanctions against Nigeria. For Washington, these included a ban on military services, bans on the sale and repair of military goods, and restrictions on visas for Nigerian government officials. Officials working West Africa in Washington scrambled to circumvent the legal restrictions as soon as they were enacted. Although there was no precedent for providing aid directly to a regional organization, procedures were quickly put in place to provide assistance to ECOMOG.

The U.S. military's ability to track and influence events in the region declined as a result of the sanctions on Nigeria. The U.S. decided not to replace the U.S. Colonel completing his tour of duty as Defense Attaché in Lagos, leaving an Air Force Major as the senior officer in the Defense Attaché Office (DAO) in Nigeria. In the downsized embassy in Monrovia, one Army Lieutenant Colonel was responsible for single-handedly covering events in both Liberia and Sierra Leone.

The policymakers' dilemma was compounded by events in Mogadishu. The divergence between American power and willpower, always apparent in Africa, became an insurmountable hurdle to military intervention on the continent after 1993. The fragile psyche of the U.S. military and foreign policy establishments, so recently buoyed by the Desert Storm experience in Iraq, was profoundly shaken. The immediate consequences of the Mogadishu tragedy were a public disillusionment with U.N. peacekeeping, and a mantra, often repeated by politicians, that the United States had no vital interests in Africa.

The U.S. military did continue to conduct short-term humanitarian, training, and non-combatant evacuation operations in Africa, but avoided committing troops as potential belligerents following the withdrawal from Somalia.[63] The decision-maker mindset change following Mogadishu was codified in Presidential Decision Directive (PDD) 25, signed by President Clinton on 3 May 1994. Replete with restrictions on future American involvement in peacekeeping, the PDD did not venture to suggest alternative modes of international conflict resolution. An exercise in policy as military force protection, the PDD's emphasis was on problem avoidance rather than problem solving. There are three basic alternatives available to the U.S. military in conflicts between third parties. It can intervene on behalf of one of the parties, conduct impartial peacekeeping, or stay out altogether. PDD 25, which made no distinction between peacekeeping and peace enforcement, tended toward the latter solution.

The two years following Mogadishu ushered in a series of personnel changes in key U.S. policy positions dealing with West Africa. In late 1994 and early 1995, Peter Chaveas, a senior State Department officer with extensive experience in Nigeria, moved on from his position as Director of the West Africa Office to become the Ambassador to Malawi. Dane Smith, who replaced him at State Department's Bureau of African Affairs

(AF), was stretched thin by his additional duties as Special Envoy for Liberia. At the NSC, dynamic political appointee Susan Rice took over the African Affairs Office.[64] The net effect of these changes was to consolidate NSC's lead on West African matters within Washington.

Significant changes were also occurring at EUCOM. In July 1995, Air Force GEN James Jamerson took over as Deputy Commander in Chief (DCINC) EUCOM.[65] From the time of GEN Jamerson's arrival, Commander in Chief, United States European Command (CINCEUR) GEN George Joulwan used him to initiate a new program of proactive engagement with African militaries.[66] Nigeria's pariah status and instability in Liberia, however, resulted in minimal EUCOM interaction with those states in the mid-1990's.[67]

U.S. assistance to ECOMOG in this time frame took discrete forms. In 1996 and 1997, the U.S. government worked through contractors to provide Nigerians in Liberia with trucks, radios, and helicopters. The U.S. behind the scenes cooperation with Nigeria's dictatorship, while clearly not in the spirit of sanctions, was nevertheless welcomed by many in Congress. [68]

Abacha's death in 1998 had a profound impact on the entire spectrum of U.S. affairs with Nigeria. It would be inaccurate, however, to assert that Abuja's sudden transition to democracy changed U.S. policy toward Nigerian regional peacekeeping. The main effect of bringing the existing relationship out into the open was to enormously increase the scale of U.S. assistance to the Nigerian military.

Susan Rice testified to Congress within days of Abacha's death regarding Nigeria's potential to "bring security to troubled neighboring states."[69] By the time U.S.

embassy personnel were evacuated from Freetown on Christmas Eve that year, a more realistic assessment of Nigerian capabilities had taken hold in Washington. [70] Special Envoy Jesse Jackson was dispatched to Sierra Leone between May and July 1999 to pressure President Ahmad Kabbah to sign a peace agreement with RUF rebels. When the Lome agreement broke down despite wholesale concessions to the RUF, the U.S. reverted to its strategy of enhanced support to the Nigerian military.

From 1999 to the present, U.S. foreign policy in West Africa has been focused on Nigeria as the region's key state. The idea behind this strategy is that limited foreign assistance resources are best spent on a state that "understands its potential regional hegemony and, more importantly, is willing and able to assert itself."[71] This anchor state strategy, which gained momentum under the Clinton administration, has been adopted by the Bush administration as well. [72] Mission Performance Guidance sent to U.S. embassies in Africa in March 2001 cites anchor states as the basis for current State Department planning.

The military assistance Nigeria has received as an anchor state has been considerable.[73] On 1 April 2000, U.S. Secretary of Defense Cohen visited Abuja and announced $10 million in aid. Of that sum, $4 million was to upgrade Nigeria's C-130's, $3.5 million was to be spent on military transformation, and $2.5 on equipment.

In July 2000, Under Secretary of State Thomas Pickering, a former ambassador to Nigeria in the early 1980s, flew to Abuja to discuss U.S. training for Nigerian troops. Operation Focus Relief, as it came to be known, involved the U.S. Third Group Special Forces providing 10 weeks training to seven battalions – five Nigerian, one Senegalese, and one Ghanaian.[74] The first three Nigerian units to receive the training were the 26th

Motorized Infantry Battalion and two composite Battalions – the 73rd Infantry Battalion and the 195th Infantry Battalion.[75] Nigerians welcomed the equipment associated with Focus Relief, but bristled at training. Citing their more extensive combat experience, the Nigerians saw little to be gained from U.S. instruction. In 2001, Nigeria pulled out of the final two scheduled Focus Relief sessions. Those will now be provided to Ghana and Senegal.[76]

The military transformation training promised the Nigerians has also proven to be a source of friction. It consists of a three-part process conducted by the American firm Military Professional Resources Incorporated (MPRI), intended to "reprofessionalize" the Nigerian Ministry of Defense. Phase one of the process, completed in 1999 at a cost to USAID of $1,000,000, entailed an assessment of actions necessary. Phase two, at a combined cost to the U.S. and Nigeria of $7 million, was initiated in late 2000. During this phase, MPRI reportedly incurred General Malu's ire by eliminating a "slush fund" he maintained. In general, the Nigerian military is showing irritation with what they perceive to be U.S. insensitivity with regard to Nigerian sovereignty. The honeymoon is over, but the strategic marriage has survived so far.

Strategic Alternatives

Events in Liberia, Sierra Leone, and Guinea are so intertwined that they cannot be addressed in the context of one nation alone. Any strategy to resolve these chronic crises must, like the crises themselves, be transnational. Peace is a necessary precursor to the creation of institutions and processes that will foster long-term stability. In a region without a tradition of inclusive government, however, ending ongoing armed conflict is only the beginning of the task at hand.

The challenge facing the international community in Sierra Leone today is how to "stop the dying" without perpetuating that nation's partition.[77] There are those who argue that military solutions produce the most lasting peace in civil wars, and negotiated settlements only sow the seeds of future conflict.[78] In the West African context, this is as irrelevant as it is true. Modern states are generally so casualty adverse that they lack the resolve necessary to conduct uncompromising war in defense of other than vital interests. Nigeria demonstrated its ability to take losses and sustain deployments over the past decade, but it was unable to resist the temptation to slip from a belligerent to a neutral role. The British have guaranteed the security of Freetown, but have not committed the forces it would take to secure all of Sierra Leone. Political will has its limits everywhere.

The U.S. has opted to treat conflict resolution in Sierra Leone primarily as an ancillary aspect of its détente with Nigeria. The fate of Nigeria, with Sub-Saharan Africa's largest population and its only mega city, is enormously important. Its embryonic democracy must be nurtured in every way, to include through the sort of military engagement the U.S. has undertaken. One should distinguish, however, between what is good for Nigeria and what is good for smaller countries in West Africa. Regional hegemons, by their nature, retard the sovereignty of weaker states in their area of influence. Nigeria, with its endemic corruption and other vestiges of its recent past, is not yet capable of instilling lasting stability in other countries.

Any lasting solution to the problems in West Africa must encompass Liberia. Although the military tool of statecraft has not proven effective to date in deterring Liberia from cross-border meddling, the Taylor regime, which has overseen a precipitous decline in Liberia's fortunes, has recently shown itself to be susceptible to economic

24

pressures.[79] A U.S. regional diplomatic offensive linking economic inducements to an end to conflict might be well received.

Whatever the approach to conflict resolution in West Africa, it must encompass all of the affected states if it is to succeed. It must also better coordinate the use of statecraft and military force, a complicated endeavor given the multiplicity of actors. A decade of Nigerian intervention has made this much clear – peacekeeping alone will not induce stability.

ENDNOTES

[1] Liberia has the highest rate of population growth in the world, with an annual increase of 4.31%. Also, globalization's impact on Taylor's revolution was considerable. While marching on Monrovia, he used a satellite phone, a novelty at the time, to maintain support and diplomatic networks around the world. See United Nations, World Population Prospects, The 2000 Revision (draft), Population Division, Department of Economic and Social Affairs, (28 February 2001), p. 56, and Herman J. Cohen, Intervening in Africa, Superpower Peacemaking in a Troubled Continent. Studies in Diplomacy (London, 2000) p.133. Also see Robert Kaplan's "The Coming Anarchy," The Atlantic Monthly (February 1994), and The Ends of the Earth: A Journey Along the Fault Lines of the Twentieth Century. Vintage Books, 1997.

[2] The Generals forced to retire endured the added indignity of having to pay back more than half the money used to train them in the course of their careers. See Kingsley Omonobi, "Army Retires 17 Generals," Vanguard Daily, (Lagos) 11 January 2001.

[3] Crossing the border from the Ivory Coast, Taylor's force initially established a stronghold in Nimba province. Doe responded by dispatching troops, drawn primarily from his Krahn minority ethnic group, to suppress the insurrection. In Nimba, the troops sent found themselves in territory home to the rival Gio tribe. The Krahns' mishandling of the local population while in pursuit of Taylor prompted a widespread rebellion, with multiple factions vying for power. Doe's rapid expansion of the army to confront the crisis led to the military absorbing criminal elements, further exacerbating abuses against civilians.

[4] Routed through Cote D'ivoire. Taylor personally took advantage of the tacit cooperation of officials in Cote D'ivoire to routinely travel overland between Liberia and Burkina Faso. Some attribute Cote D'ivoire's decision to assist the NPFL to the murder of Liberian President Tolbert when Doe took power. Tolbert's wife Daisy was an adopted daughter of Cote D'ivoire President Felix Houphouet-Boigny.

[5] Funmi Olonisakin. Reinventing Peacekeeping in Africa – Conceptual and Legal Issues in ECOMOG Operations. (London, 2000), p. 93.

[6] The deployment was actually ordered by The Standing Mediation Committee of ECOWAS.

[7] Using a variety of civilian aircraft and sea vessels in addition to military transport, ECOMOG initially deployed to a base in Freetown, Sierra Leone. From there, small patrol craft moved troops on to Monrovia. ECOMOG would sustain about 150 logistics personnel in Sierra Leone, at staging areas at Lungi airport and the Freetown port, for the seven-year duration of the Liberian conflict.

[8] Original in Pidgin.

[9] In theory, ECOMOG troops were each due five dollars per diem a day from their respective governments.

[10] Dennis Jett. Why Peacekeeping Fails. (New York, 1999), p. 134.

[11] One diplomat noted "By the time the Nigerians really got serious about bringing this war to an end…they had taken just about everything that there was to take from Liberia." See Kenneth Cain, "Meanwhile in Africa", SAIS Review, (Winter/Spring 2000), p. 153-176.

[12] Eghosa E.Osaghae, Crippled Giant, Nigeria Since Independence. (Indiana University Press, 1998), p. 269.

[13] Vanguard Daily, Lagos, 19 January 2001.

[14] Reuters, 10 April 2001.

[15] At Koindu in the north and at the Mano River Bridge in the south. See Earl Conteh-Morgan and Mac Dixon-Fyle. Sierra Leone at the End of the Twentieth Century (New York, 1999), p. 127.

[16] United Nations Panel of Exports Report on Diamonds and Arms in Sierra Leone. 20 December 2000, paragraph 180.

[17] The Strasser coup brought 24 years of All Peoples Congress rule in Sierra Leone to an end. Sierra Leone's ruler at the time of the coup, Major General Joseph Momoh, was ill equipped to handle the RUF challenge. Since assuming office in an unopposed election in 1985, he had proven unable to reverse a general decline in the country's fortunes. Hosting a flood of refugees fleeing the Liberian war had exacerbated Sierra Leone's woes, as had the implementation of economic reform measures demanded by the International Monetary Fund.

[18] Conteh, op. cit., p. 135.

[19] Charles Dokubo. "'An Army for Rent', Private Military Corporations and Civil Conflicts in Africa: The Case of Sierra Leone". Civil Wars, vol. 3, No. 2 (Summer 2000), pp 58-59.

[20] The roots of the 1997 coup lay in Sierra Leone's ethnic and institutional politics. Kabbah, an ethnic Mende from the southeast, was perceived by many to favor his own people. His appointment of fellow Mende Hinga Norman as Deputy Minister of Defense was particularly threatening to the military. Norman was a former Chief of the Kamajor local militias in the southeast. These militias had fought the RUF much more effectively over time than had the discredited Army. Under Kabbah, state resources were increasingly diverted from the Army to the Kamajors. The rivalry between the groups was such that battles were fought between them prior to the coup. Koroma, in justifying his coup, specifically cited purported Kabbah favoritism toward the Kamajors. Following the coup, the Kamajors remained loyal to the ousted government and continued to fight both the RUF and the Army. Their leader, "Sam" Hinga Norman, is representative of a web of shadowy ties that connect actors on all sides of the region's conflicts. Although publicly opposed to the RUF, he quietly spent extensive periods of time in Monrovia in the months following the coup. His ability to do so safely suggests a private accommodation with the forces he opposed. See Conteh, op. cit., pg. 137-147 for related information.

[21] A substantial number of Nigerian troops had been in Sierra Leone conducting bilateral training at time of the coup. One of two battalions dedicated to that task had just rotated out, reaching Monrovia en route to Nigeria the day of the coup. The poor showing of the Nigerians remaining in Sierra Leone in fighting AFRC/RUF coalition cost the Nigerian commander on the ground his position.

[22] Nigerian Brigadier General A. Mohammed organized the initial effort in April 1997. Force Commander Lieutenant General Victor Malu, who would normally have been in charge, was away in Nigeria at the time. Malu's return to Monrovia inexplicably took weeks, leaving Mohammed in de facto command during the difficult early stages of the operation.

[23] Lieutenant General Malu was ECOMOG Chief of Staff and Director of Operations from 1992 to 1993. He had received high marks from outside observers for his tough stance in dealing with Charles Taylor previously, both in his capacity as ECOMOG Force Commander and as ECOMOG Chief of Staff.

[24] Its substance consisted of themes that would resonate in future such agreements, to include the demobilization of combatants, international financial assistance, power sharing within the government, and unconditional immunities from prosecution. Also of note, the agreement called for the return of RUF leader Foday Sankoh to Sierra Leone. Sankoh had been arrested in Nigeria in March 1997 on charges of arms smuggling.

[25] Diplomats accredited to Sierra Leone in 1998 speak of how hard it was to sustain the delusion that they were dealing with a host government. Kabbah was so dependent on outside assistance that, at one point, his regime generated only $400 a quarter in domestic revenue. By August 1999, Government of Sierra Leone income was up to $7,000 a month. See related information in Jonathan Rauch, "Two Cheers for the Clinton Doctrine. (OK, Maybe Just One)." National Journal, vol. 32, no. 22 (27 May 2000), p. 2.

[26] Major General Vijay Kumar Jetley's unpublished memo to the UN, available at http://www.sierra-leone.org/jetley0500.html

[27] Sam Bockarie, a former diamond digger who became the RUF/AFRC Chief of Defense Staff, had a falling out with Koroma over diamonds during the RUF retreat from Freetown in late 1998. A subsequent dispute between Bockarie and Sankoh over diamonds led to the former's exile in Liberia. See the UN Report on Diamonds, op. cit. paragraphs 72-77.

[28] Ibid., paragraphs 183-184.

[29] "Saving Sierra Leone, At a Price," The New York Times, 4 February 1999.

[30] John R. Bolton, "United States Policy on United Nations Peacekeeping." World Affairs, vol. 163, no. 3 (Washington, Winter 2001) pp. 129-147.

[31] "U.N. Monitors Accuse Sierra Leone Peacekeepers of Killings," The New York Times, 12 February 1999.

[32] In March 1999, Nigerian Major General Timothy Shelpidi was abruptly recalled to Nigeria after only one year as ECOMOG Commander. The newly democratic government in Abuja under General Obasanjo apparently felt it necessary to take some action in the wake of embarrassments in Sierra Leone. Major General Shelpidi receives Generally poor reviews from Westerners who knew him. Despite superficially impressive qualifications for his position, to include experience in Liberia, fluency in Creole, and a diplomatic manner, Shelpidi was unable to put his abilities to effective use in Sierra Leone. Some characterize him as "a real weakling," soft spoken without charisma, and uncomfortable with the technical aspects of operations. Shelpidi's two top aides, Brigadier General Abu Ahmadu and Brigadier General Gabriel Kpamber, were recalled with him. The new democratic government in Abuja reportedly made the

decision to replace Shelpidi following consultations with British Foreign Secretary Robin Cook. See "Why General Shelpidi Was Fired" in New African, May 1999.

[33] Peace Agreement Between the Government of Sierra Leone and the Revolutionary United Front of Sierra Leone, at Sierra Leone.org/lomeaccord.html.

[34] The U.N. was awarded the Nobel Peace Prize on 11 December 1988 for it peacekeeping activities.

[35] Dennis Jett. Why Peacekeeping Fails. (New York, 1999), p.18.

[36] Jett, op. cit.

[37] The Secretary General's meetings with regional organizations took place in New York in 1994 and 1996. See William Lewis and Edward Marks. Searching for Partners: Regional Organizations and Peace Operations. McNair Paper 58. Institute for National Strategic Studies, National Defense University, Washington DC, June 1998. Also see Final Report on the In-Depth Evaluation of Peacekeeping Operation: Start Up Phase. UN Office of Oversight Services, 17 March 1995, paragraph 12.

[38] Boutros-Ghali was aware of some of the hazards entailed in courting regional powers. He noted: "War in one country may get enormous attention, while war elsewhere may be virtually ignored…. These latter conflicts are orphans, deprived of international attention, concern, and effort. They demand and deserve that the international community commit the needed political, financial, humanitarian, civil, and, in some cases, military resources….As Secretary General I have actively sought the involvement of regional arrangements and agencies…. Authorization to serve as a surrogate might strengthen a particular power's sphere of influence and damage the United Nations' standing as an organization intended to coordinate security across regional blocs. The overuse of authorization and delegation may also damage the United Nations' image, and the public may fail to understand why the world organization is not directly engaged in addressing the problems. Above all, these methods of coping with the increasing demands on the United Nations raise the danger of overreliance on a particular state or group of states, undermining the principle of universality." See Boutros Boutros-Ghali. "Global Leadership After the Cold War." Foreign Affairs, vol. 75, no. 2, (March/April 1996), pp 86-99.

[39] Some of Boutros-Ghali's orphan conflicts received U.N. attention when the decline in peacekeeping experienced from 1994 through 1998 was reversed in the final two years of the twentieth century. Operations in Kosovo (UNMIK), East Timor (UNTAET), the Democratic Republic of Congo (MONOC), Ethiopia/Eritrea (UNMEE), and Sierra Leone heralded a new era. The U.N. took on neo-colonial responsibilities in UNMIK and UNTAET, filling governmental vacuums in the aftermath of de facto secessions. Both operations are open-ended, with no hope of near-term closure. The situations that MONOC and UNAMSIL face reveal that the evolution of war in Africa has outpaced U.N.'s capacity to contend with it. The respect for the permanency of territorial borders that once was common among Africa's leaders has dissipated. War represents a challenge for peacekeeping forces, which tend to exhibit a proclivity for negotiation. The presence of U.N. troops has unavoidably partisan consequences in areas alternating between ceasefires and combat. It sustains combatants, draws out the resolution of conflict, and ultimately proves counterproductive. See "The UN's Missions Impossible," The Economist, (3 August 2000). Also, Cain, op. cit. who succinctly notes that in modern peacekeeping, regional hegemons want in, the U.S. wants out, and the U.N. wants credit.

[40] Bolton, op. cit. UNOMSIL was typical of the smaller U.N. missions undertaken in the mid-1990's, sending only 41 personnel to Sierra Leone initially. See Jett, op. cit., p.4.

[41] See Conteh, op. cit., pg. 137-147. In early 1999, Nigerian Major General Kpamber traveled to New York to discuss taking on U.N. responsibilities. In New York, he was informed that the Nigerian contingent of UNAMSIL would be subordinated to the overall direction of Mission Commander Major General Jetley. The Nigerian military took the selection of an Indian to Command the mission as an affront, and asserted that Nigerian sacrifices in Sierra Leone warranted the selection of a Nigerian officer. Relations between

the Nigerian and Indian military contingents in Sierra Leone would remain strained throughout the Indians' participation in the operation. Kpamber, who was recalled with Shelpidi, was also later implicated in illegal diamond mining with the RUF.

[42] Primarily Zambians.

[43] A.J. Venter, "Taking Control in Sierra Leone," Jane's International Defense Review, vol. 33,No. 9, (1 September 2000).

[44] Preston, Anthony. "British Intervention Poses Question: A Precedent, Or One-Time Exception?" Sea Power. (Washington, July 2000).

[45] Indeed, there had been a British Military Assistance Team (BMAT) on the ground in Freetown three years earlier at time of the May 1997 coup.

[46] For details, see New African, op. cit.

[47] "Sierra Leone: A Tumultuous Year," The Economist, (27 December 2000).

[48] "British Troops Will Strike In 24 Hours – Geof Hoon," Standard Times, (2 February 2001).

[49] Not all of the contributing militaries in UNAMSIL were capable of making the transition. Many smaller developing nation militaries have become so specialized in peacekeeping (which earns state revenues), that they are not particularly adept at actual warfare.

[50] Pakistanis have since pledged to replace some of the departing peacekeepers.

[51] "Sierra Leone Rebels Contemplate Life Without Guns," The Washington Post, 14 April 2001, p. A1.

[52] "West Africa States Try to Head Off Regional War," Reuters. 10 April 2001.

[53] "Sierra Leone Rebels Contemplate Life Without Guns," op. cit., p. A14.

[54] "Fear of Clashes Following Liberian Call-Up," Johannesburg Star. 9 April 2001.

[55] Article 52 of the U.N. Charter, which addresses regional arrangements, makes allowances for action against "enemy states," but makes no reference to civil wars. Article 52 of the Charter encourages the peaceful settlement of disputes, but allows for regional organization enforcement actions provided specific Security Council authorities are granted.

[56] Roy Licklider. "The Consequences of Negotiated Settlements in Civil Wars, 1945-1993." The American political Science Review, (September 1995), p 681-692.

[57] See Lakdar Brahimi (ed.), Report of the Panel on United Nations Peace Operations, (UN, 21 August 2000).

[58] According to Cohen, op. cit., p. 134, the CIA argued protection of its communications link in Liberia was "vital." Cain, op. cit. reports the CIA Station in Monrovia primarily targeted Libya and Angola.

[59] Olonisakin, op. cit. p. 93-94.

[60] Cohen. Op. cit. p. 10, 139-144.

[61] Timothy Andrews. "Dysfunctional Equilibrium, U.S. Policy Toward Nigeria, 1995-1997." National War College unpublished paper, Fort McNair, Washington DC, 1998. p. 2.

[62] Cohen, op. cit., p. 161.

[63] The Americans were not alone in their change of heart. The French, with a much longer and more active history of intervention on the continent, fundamentally changed their policy in 1995. In announcing its *Renforcement des Capacites Africianes de Maintien de la Paix* (RECAMP) program to arm and train selected African Francophone states to address African conflicts, the French government indicated that it would no longer unilaterally intervene in Africa. A new policy of "no indifference – no insurance" distanced the French from their former colonies in West Africa.

[64] Timothy Andrews. op. cit. pp. 1-4.

[65] Ambassador Chaveas later joined GEN Jamerson in Stuttgart as the Political Advisor to EUCOM.

[66] General Jamerson oversaw an unprecedented number of EUCOM bilateral activities with African militaries, encompassing a wide array of exercises, training, and visit exchanges between senior officers. A proposal to realize GEN Joulwan's vision of a "Marshall Center for Africa" was also put into motion, which eventually resulted in the creation of the African Center for Strategic Studies. Of perhaps even greater significance, GEN Joulwan gained approval for a plan to establish 18 new DAO's in Africa over five fiscal years - including plans to establish a DAO in Freetown, which have been put on indefinite hold.

[67] A EUCOM Joint Combined Exchange Training (JCET) team was coincidentally in Freetown at the time of the 1997 Koroma coup, and assisted in the evacuation of U.S. personnel. In 1997, EUCOM expanded its already broad range of cooperation with African militaries by introducing the African Crisis Response Initiative (ACRI). Under that program, U.S. soldiers provided non-lethal peacekeeping training to select African militaries, to prepare them for potentially conducting peacekeeping missions under the auspices of Chapter 6 of the U.N. Charter. Conspicuously absent from the list of ACRI partner states were the continent's two major powers – Nigeria and South Africa.

[68] The dichotomy was apparent at a Hearing in 1997. Testimony was presented regarding an independent watchdog organization's rating of Nigeria as the most corrupt country in the world. This was followed by a separate report on dissident Nigerian soldiers winding up killed or missing in action in Liberia. After hearing all this, Congressman William J. Jefferson advocated "enlisting Nigeria's cooperation and assistance on a range of regional and international issues, including peacekeeping and regional stability." Acting Secretary of State for Africa Johnnie Carson, noting sanctions banning military sales and assistance to Nigeria, testified, "As a major player in the U.N. and the current chairman of…ECOWAS, Nigeria can be a valuable partner on regional initiatives of mutual interest. We and Nigeria worked effectively on the Liberian peace process….We seek similar cooperation with Nigeria on the current crisis in Sierra Leone."18 Sept 1997, Hearing before the subcommittee on Africa of the House of Representatives Committee on International Relations on US Policy Toward Nigeria. Also see Transparency International's The Year 2000 Corruption Perceptions Index, at http://www.transparency.de/documents/cpi/2000/cpi2000 html.

[69] Susan Rice's 26 June 1998 testimony before the House of Representatives Committee on International Relations.

[70] The newly appointed Ambassador to Sierra Leone had arrived only a month earlier, in November 1998. Within ten days of the NEO, RUF entered Freetown.

[71] Senator Frist at 1 May 2000 Committee on Foreign Relations Hearing – See http:www.nato50.org/lagos/wwwhcf03 html

[72] President George W. Bush's approach toward U.S. involvement in Africa's conflicts was previewed in a statement he made as a candidate in February 2000; "I didn't like what went on in Rwanda, but I don't think we should commit troops to Rwanda. Nor do I think that we ought to try to be the peacekeepers all around the world. I intend to tell our allies that America will help make the peace, but you get to put troops on the ground to keep warring parties apart."

[73] $600,000 in International Military Education Training (IMET) funds were also set aside for Nigeria in Fiscal Year (FY) 2000, and $860,000 in FY 2001.

[74] In contrast to the ACRI program, which the Nigerians continue to shun, Focus Relief does provide lethal training. Section 564 of the Foreign Operations, Export Financing, and Related Programs Appropriations Act of 2000 and related provisions in the Defense Appropriations Act of 1997, known as the "Leahy Amendment" require the U.S. embassy to check Nigerians backgrounds for human rights abuses before training is allowed. Actual vetting capability is limited. While ECOMOG abuses in Liberia and Sierra Leone are recorded and units sometimes identified, individual perpetrators of human rights abuses are seldom known.

[75] "US Army Donates Equipment to Nigeria Military," Panafrican News Agency, 27 December 2000.

[76] In budgeting for Focus relief training, JCET in the rest of Africa was cut back.

[77] Transnational rebel groups sustained by outside actors are unfortunately not unique to West Africa. International borders in much of the world have gone from inviolable to inviable in recent years. The dispatch of peacekeeping troops, with their imperative to arrest conflict without assigning blame, can do more harm than good in resolving such situations. The partition of countries often takes on an unacknowledged permanence under U.N. tutelage. The instigators of instability are rewarded with territory, and foreign soldiers sustain weak governments. Afghanistan, Angola, Bosnia, the Democratic Republic of Congo, Georgia, Rwanda, and Sudan, among others, have been victims of prolonged civil wars over the past decade. Stronger states, such as the United States, Russia, South Africa and Serbia, have invariably been behind sustaining such conflicts. For commentary on this phenomenon within an African context, see Cohen op. cit. p 323-325. Colombia is an interesting variant on this trend. Cocaine production there parallels West African diamond digging as an activity that fuels conflict between transnational rebels and weak states, while also inducing corruption. Although Colombian rebels flow freely across the borders of neighboring states, they do not appear to be reliant on a single foreign sponsor.

[78] See Edward Luttwak. "Give War a Chance", Foreign Affairs, vol. 78, no. 4, (July/August 1999), pp 36-44, and also see Roy Licklider. "The Consequences of Negotiated Settlements in Civil Wars, 1945-1993." The American political Science Review, (September 1995), p 681-692.

[79] For example, Taylor's reactions to the imposition of economic sanctions related to the export of Sierra Leonean diamonds.

Bibliography

Adedeji, Adebayo (ed.). <u>Comprehending and Mastering African Conflicts</u>, (New York, 1999).

Andrews, Timothy. "Dysfunctional Equilibrium, U.S. Policy Toward Nigeria, 1995-1997." National War College unpublished paper, Fort McNair, Washington DC, 1998.

Bolton, John R. "United States Policy on United Nations Peacekeeping." <u>World Affairs</u>, vol. 163, no. 3 (Washington, Winter 2001).

Boutros-Ghali, Boutros. "Global Leadership After the Cold War." <u>Foreign Affairs</u>, vol. 75, no. 2, (March/April 1996), pp 86-99.

Brahimi, Lakdar (ed.), <u>Report of the Panel on United Nations Peace Operations</u>, (UN, 21 August 2000).

Cain, Kenneth. "Meanwhile in Africa," <u>SAIS Review</u> (Winter/Spring 2000).

Clough, Michael. <u>Free at Last? U.S. Policy Toward Africa and the End of the Cold War</u>. Council on Foreign Relations Press (New York, 1992).

Cohen, Herman J. <u>Intervening in Africa, Superpower Peacemaking in a Troubled Continent</u>. Studies in Diplomacy (London, 2000).

Conteh-Morgan, Earl and Mac Dixon-Fyle. <u>Sierra Leone at the End of the Twentieth Century</u>. New York: Lang Publishing, 1999.

Cook, Nicholas. <u>U.S. Military Training of West African Forces for Peacekeeping</u>. Congressional Research Service, 28 August 2000.

Copley, Gregory. "Deal With Africa's Cancers, Not Symptoms," <u>Defense and Foreign Affairs Strategic Policy</u>, vol. 28, no. 8 (August 2000).

Dagne, Theodros. <u>Nigeria in Political Transition</u>. Congressional Research Service Report for Congress (17 July 2000).

Dokubo, Charles. "'An Army for Rent', Private Military Corporations and Civil Conflicts in Africa: The Case of Sierra Leone". Civil Wars, vol. 3, No. 2 (Summer 2000), pp 51-64.

Ekwe-Ekwe, Herbert. Conflict and Intervention in Africa. (New York, 1990).

Fact Sheet: U.S.-Nigerian Cooperation on Peacekeeping and Military Reform. U.S. Department of State (26 August 2000).

Geddes, John. "The Price of Peacekeeping." Maclean's, (Toronto, 12 February 2001).

House of Representatives. Hearing before the Subcommittee on Africa of the Committee on International Relations. 18 September 1997.

Jett, Dennis Jett. Why Peacekeeping Fails. (New York, 1999).

Joint Publication 3-0, Doctrine for Joint Operations, (Final Coordination 5 February 2001).

Joint Publication 3-07, Joint Doctrine for Military Operations Other Than War, (16 June 1995).

Joint Publication 3-07.3, Joint Tactics, Techniques, and Procedures for Peace Operations, (12 February 1999).

Kabbah, Ahmad Tejan. Address to British Trained "B" Battalion of the Sierra Leone Army at the Benguema Training Center, (5 April 2001).

Kaplan, Robert. "The Coming Anarchy," The Atlantic Monthly (February 1994).

Kaplan, Robert. The Ends of the Earth: A Journey Along the Fault Lines of the Twentieth Century. Vintage Books, 1997.

Lewis, William and Edward Marks. Searching for Partners: Regional Organizations and Peace Operations. McNair Paper 58. Institute for National Strategic Studies, National Defense University, Washington DC, June 1998.

Licklider, Roy. The Consequences of Negotiated Settlements in Civil Wars, 1945-1993. The American political Science Review, (September 1995), p 681-692.

Lizza, Ryan. "Sierra Leone, The Last Clinton Betrayal. Where Angels Fear to Tread." The New Republic, (July 2000).

Luttwak, Edward. "Give War a Chance", Foreign Affairs, vol. 78, no. 4, (July/August 1999), pp 36-44.

McGreal, Chris, "Nigerian UN Troops Accused of Corruption." The Guardian (11 September 2000).

"Memorandum on Emergency Military Assistance to the United Nations Mission in Sierra Leone," Weekly Compilation of Presidential Documents, Washington, 18 December 2000.

"Nigerian Army Denies Misappropriating Peacekeeping Funds." Pan African News Agency (5 July 2000).

"Nigerian Army Head Demands the Removal of General Jetley." The Times of India (14 September 2000).

Olonisakin, Funmi. Reinventing Peacekeeping in Africa – Conceptual and Legal Issues in ECOMOG Operations. (London, 2000).

Osaghae, Eghosa, E. Crippled Giant, Nigeria Since Independence. (Indiana University Press, 1998).

1

Overseas Development Council. U.S. Policy Toward the New Democratic Government of Nigeria: Summary of Policy Roundtable Discussions. ODC Policy Program at www.odc.org/commentary/nigeria.html

Preston, Anthony. "British Intervention Poses Question: A Precedent, Or One-Time Exception?" Sea Power. (Washington, July 2000).

Rauch, Jonathan. "Two Cheers for the Clinton Doctrine. (OK, Maybe Just One)." National Journal, vol. 32, no. 22 (27 May 2000).

Rice, Susan. Statement to House of Representatives Committee on International Relations. 25 June 1998.

Rotberg, Robert, Ericka Albaugh, Happyton Bonyongwe, Christopher Clapham, Jeffrey Herbst, and Steven Metz. Peacekeeping and Peace Enforcement in Africa. Brookings Institution Press (Washington DC, 2000).

"Sierra Leone: A Tumultuous Year," The Economist, (27 December 2000).

Stremlau, John. "Ending Africa's Wars", Foreign Affairs, vol. 79, no. 4, (July/August 2000), pp 117-132.

The White House. A National Security Strategy for a New Century. (Washington DC, December 1999).

Transparency International. 2000 Corruption Perceptions Index, (Berlin, September 2000).

Transparency International. The Precision and Regional Comparison of Perceived Levels of Corruption – Interpreting the Results. (Berlin, September 2000).

"U.S. Army Donates Equipment to Nigerian Military." Pan African News Agency (27 December 2000).

United States European Command. Strategy of Readiness and Engagement, (Stuttgart, Germany, 1998). Available from <http://www.eucom.mil/strategy.html>.

United Nations Panel of Exports Report on Diamonds and Arms in Sierra Leone. 20 December 2000.

"The UN's Missions Impossible," The Economist, (3 August 2000).

U.S. Senate. Nigerian Transition and the Future of U.S. Policy. Hearing 4 November 1999.

Venter, AJ. "Taking Control in Sierra Leone," Jane's International Defense Review, vol. 33,No. 9, (1 September 2000).

Vesely, Milan. "UN Peacekeepers: Warriors or Victims?" African Business, vol. 261 (London, January 2001).

"Why General Shelpidi Was Fired," New African, (3 September 2001).